HISTORY IN PICTURES

FOCUS ON
CIVIL RIGHTS SIT-INS

CICELY LEWIS

Lerner Publications ◆ Minneapolis

LETTER FROM CICELY LEWIS

Dear Reader,

Imagine being in an argument with a classmate and the teacher asks what happened. Your classmate tells their version of the story, but you don't get to share your version. Do you think this is fair? Well, this is what has happened throughout history.

CICELY LEWIS

This series looks at different events in US history with a focus on photos that help tell stories of people from underrepresented groups.

I started the Read Woke challenge in response to the needs of my students. I wanted my students to read books that challenged social norms and shared perspectives from underrepresented and oppressed groups. I created Read Woke Books because I want you to be knowledgeable and compassionate citizens.

As you look through these books, think about the photos that have captured history. Why are they important? What do they teach you? I hope you learn from these books and get inspired to make our world a better place for all.

Yours in solidarity,

—Cicely Lewis, Executive Editor

TABLE OF CONTENTS

Think critically about the photos throughout this book. Who is taking the photos and why? What is their viewpoint? Who are the people in the photos? What do these photos tell us?

There are so many important people and events in the civil rights movement, and we are not able to include them all in this book. After finishing this book, learn more about the movement. There are tips on page 25 to help you get started.

Left to right: John Salter Jr., Joan Trumpauer, and Anne Moody sit at the Woolworth lunch counter in Jackson, Mississippi, in protest. Salter was covered in food by the angry mob.

SITTING TO TAKE A STAND

ON MAY 28, 1963, ANNE MOODY, MEMPHIS NORMAN, AND PEARLENA LEWIS—BLACK STUDENTS FROM TOUGALOO COLLEGE—SAT AT WOOLWORTH LUNCH COUNTER IN JACKSON, MISSISSIPPI. Woolworth was a department store chain that also had a lunch counter. But there was one problem: Woolworth allowed Black shoppers, but they forbid Black people from eating at the lunch counter.

That day the three students, as well as white Tougaloo College student Joan Trumpauer, white professor John Salter Jr., and others, sat at the counter to take a stand against racial injustice.

A white mob poured food on the demonstrators from Tougaloo, called them names and used racist language, and physically attacked them. Moody later wrote in her autobiography *Coming of Age in Mississippi* that the mob slapped her face and threw Norman off his seat. Despite the mob's attacks, the group refused to leave. Their sit-in was a part of a large youth-led movement to challenge racial injustice.

Anne Moody in the 1970s

On April 23, 1956, Black and white passengers are segregated on an Atlanta Transit Company bus.

CHAPTER 1
BEGINNING THE CIVIL RIGHTS MOVEMENT

THE CIVIL RIGHTS MOVEMENT STARTED IN THE MID-1950S AND ENDED IN THE LATE 1960S. Although slavery ended decades earlier, Black people still faced discrimination and segregation. During the civil rights movement, many people protested to demand equal rights for Black people.

On March 2, 1955, fifteen-year-old Claudette Colvin was riding on a segregated bus. When she was asked to give up her seat for a white person, she refused and was arrested.

Nine months later, Rosa Parks was arrested for refusing to give up her seat too. Parks had already been working as a civil rights activist for years and worked with organizations and Black leaders that fought for the rights of Black people.

These two women, as well as others, sparked the Montgomery Bus Boycott. From December 5, 1955, to December 20, 1956, many Black people in Montgomery, Alabama, protested segregation by refusing to ride city buses. In November 1956 the US Supreme Court upheld a federal district court ruling that segregation on public buses was unconstitutional. Montgomery had to integrate its bus system.

Claudette Colvin in 1953

Rosa Parks after arrest in 1955

JIM CROW AND SEGREGATION

From the 1870s to the 1960s, Jim Crow laws limited the rights of Black people. Some laws sought to keep Black people separated from white people. This kind of segregation was upheld by the Supreme Court through the idea of "separate but equal" for Black and white people. In reality, public places for Black people were not equal to those for white people. Public places like restaurants, schools, and drinking fountains were segregated. Jim Crow and legalized segregation ended with the rise of the civil rights movement and activists.

REFLECT

Colored is an out-of-date term that was used to refer to Black people. Why do you think we no longer use this term?

A Black man and a white man drink out of segregated drinking fountains.

FOR COLORED ONLY

Other forms of protest occurred, such as the protests of the Freedom Riders. Freedom Riders were groups of people who protested segregated bus terminals. On May 4, 1961, thirteen Freedom Riders boarded a Greyhound bus to the South. There, the Freedom Riders were met by an angry mob of white people who threw a bomb onto the bus and beat them. When the riders reached Jackson, Mississippi, they were arrested. But hundreds of people, including activists Diane Nash and John Lewis, joined the cause and the rides continued.

Many other people and events were instrumental to the civil rights movement. All of them helped to change history.

On May 19, 1961, a group of Freedom Riders from Tennessee wait to board a Greyhound bus in Birmingham, Alabama, a segregated bus terminal.

Protesters have a sit-in at a segregated lunch counter in Arlington, Virginia, in 1960. White protesters hold up signs criticizing and mocking the sit-in and racial equality.

CHAPTER 2
WOOLWORTH LUNCH COUNTER SIT-INS

On February 1, 1960, four Black college students, Joseph McNeil, Ezell Blair Jr. (now known as Jibreel Khazan), Franklin McCain, and David Richmond, went to the Woolworth store in Greensboro, North Carolina. After buying school supplies, the students went to the lunch counter to sit and eat. They refused to give up their seats after they were asked to leave.

Franklin McCain (*left*) and David Richmond (*right*) in April 1960, two months after their sit-in in Greensboro

News of the Greensboro sit-in spread. The Greensboro Four, as McNeil, Blair, McCain, and Richmond came to be known, started a movement for others to stand up for justice. The Greensboro Four kept going back to Woolworth day after day. Each day, more people joined them. The number of people participating rose to four hundred. The action of the Greensboro Four also inspired students in other cities and states to stage sit-ins, such as Anne Moody's sit-in.

"Fifteen seconds after I sat on that stool, I had the most wonderful feeling. I had a feeling of liberation," McCain later said about the sit-in. "And I truly felt almost invincible."

Left to right: Joseph McNeil, David Richmond, Franklin McCain, and Jabreel Khazan sit at the Woolworth lunch counter in Greensboro on February 1, 1980, the twentieth anniversary of their sit-in.

REFLECT

Why is it important to protest racial injustice? Compare the risks of protesting with the risks of staying quiet.

College students were a driving force behind sit-ins. Historically Black colleges and universities (HBCUs) became centers for equality and justice. The participation of HBCU students was instrumental to the success of the civil rights movement. Many became some of the movement's greatest leaders, including Martin Luther King Jr., Medgar Evers, and Rosa Parks. HBCU students held meetings in their dorm rooms or chapel basements.

In 1962 in Georgia, members of the SNCC stand by the ruins of Mount Mary Baptist Church, one of the Black churches destroyed in a series of racial attacks.

CHAPTER 3
COLLEGE STUDENTS LEAD THE WAY

THE CIVIL RIGHTS MOVEMENT WAS FUELED BY YOUNG ADULTS. In 1960 the Student Nonviolent Coordinating Committee (SNCC) was founded. The SNCC gave young activists more voice and leadership in the civil rights movement. It also worked on civil rights campaigns.

Students from Fisk University led boycotts and marches that helped end segregation in Nashville, Tennessee. In 1957 students from Knoxville College in Knoxville, Tennessee,

On June 24, 1964, students attend a class at Western College in Oxford, Ohio. The goal of the class was to prepare them to help with Black voter registration in Mississippi.

started one of the first voter registration drives to help lead desegregation efforts.

On March 27, 1961, nine Black students entered Jackson Municipal Public Library, a segregated library, in Mississippi. They intended to protest the library's discrimination. They were Tougaloo College students Joseph Jackson Jr., Geraldine Edwards, James "Sammy" Bradford, Evelyn Pierce, Albert Lassiter, Ethel Sawyer, Meredith Anding Jr., Janice Jackson, and Alfred Cook.

After entering the library, which was reserved for white people, Edwards went to the library assistant's desk and asked for a book. She was told that the library could only be accessed by white people. The book was not available at the George Washington Carver Library, the only library Black people in Jackson were allowed to use. Although the assistant told her to leave, she and the other students sat down and began to read. Police arrested the Tougaloo Nine after they refused to leave the library. They were charged with disturbing public peace.

Members of the Tougalou Nine, *left to right*: (*top row*) Joseph Jackson Jr., Albert Lassiter, Alfred Cook, James Bradford, Janice Jackson, (*bottom row*) Ethel Sawyer, Geraldine Edwards, Evelyn Pierce, and Meredith Anding Jr.

MARCH ON WASHINGTON

On August 28, 1963, around 250,000 people met at Lincoln Memorial in Washington, DC. The crowd gathered for the March on Washington, also known as the March on Washington for Jobs and Freedom,

Martin Luther King Jr. addresses the crowd at the Lincoln Memorial during the March on Washington.

Marchers hold up signs to protest for voting rights, jobs, and an end to police brutality during the March on Washington.

to protest discrimination and inequality. Many people spoke at the event, including Martin Luther King Jr. who gave his famous "I Have a Dream" speech.

Their act sparked protests from students at Jackson State University and other nearby colleges. Victory came the following year when the American Library Association said that members must welcome everyone, regardless of race and religion.

In 1964 nearly one thousand student volunteers from across the country traveled to the Mississippi Delta in the South to encourage Black voter registration and to stop discrimination at the polls. This movement was called

Left to right (front row): David McDermott, Patricia Hoskins, and Ryujiro Iseda study in the integrated library at Tougaloo College on March 22, 1965.

"When people talk about nonviolence, they think of a sort of passivity, a peacefulness. If you are talking about the Civil Rights Movement and our practice of nonviolence, you have to think of aggressive, confrontational activity . . . nonviolent actions to force change."

—BERNICE JOHNSON REAGON,
singer, activist, and founding member of the SNCC

Freedom Summer, or Mississippi Summer Project. In the South, the Ku Klux Klan (a white supremacy group) and law enforcement members confronted, beat, and arrested the volunteers. Black volunteer James Chaney and white volunteers Michael Schwerner and Andrew Goodman were murdered. These activities, and the actions of others, led to the Voting Rights Act of 1965.

Tyra Hemans (*with microphone*), Emma González (*holding Hemans's hand*), and other students from Marjory Stoneman Douglas High School speak at March for Our Lives in 2018.

CHAPTER 4
STUDENT AND YOUTH ACTIVISM

THE PEOPLE AND EVENTS OF THE CIVIL RIGHTS MOVEMENT CONTINUE TO INSPIRE YOUTH-LED ACTIVISM. Young people continue the tradition of protests. They protest climate change, gun violence, discrimination, police brutality, and more.

After a gunman killed seventeen people at Marjory Stoneman Douglas High School in Florida on February 14, 2018, students decided to take action. They wanted to see laws to address gun violence. On March 24 they marched on Washington. The historic march for gun control was called March for Our Lives.

On June 4, 2020, the six teenagers who founded Teens 4 Equality—Nya Collins, Jade Fuller, Kennedy Green, Emma Rose Smith, Mikayla Smith, and Zee Thomas—led a march of ten thousand peaceful protesters in Nashville. The teenagers organized the youth march against police violence on social media. In response, Nashville mayor John Cooper announced that all police officers would wear body cameras.

"As teens, we feel we cannot make a difference in this world, but we must," Zee said.

Teens 4 Equality organizers speak at their protest against police violence on June 4, 2020.

REFLECT

During a rally on May 31, 2020, protesters reflect on the death of George Floyd, a Black man who was killed by a white police officer in Minneapolis, Minnesota, six days earlier.

"I do believe in the future because there are a lot of kids who are changing the future, trying to end white supremacy and hatred and racism in America."

—KENNEDY GREEN,
founding member of Teens 4 Equality

TAKE ACTION

You can take action and speak out against injustices. Let your voice be heard! Here are some ways to get started:

Start a little free library in your neighborhood, and include books by and featuring people of color.

Explore the Civil Rights History Project to learn about ways activists brought about change during the civil rights movement and get inspired to make change. You can watch the interviews at https://www.loc.gov /collections/civil-rights-history-project/?fa=subject :interviews&sb=shelf-id_desc. Some of the videos also have transcripts of the interviews that you can read.

Attend your school board meetings, and ask to speak about issues in your school that concern you.

Research youth-led groups or movements such as Fridays for Future and March for Our Lives. Learn how to get involved, and speak out for the topics you care about.

TIMELINE

MARCH 2, 1955 — Claudette Colvin is arrested after refusing to give up her seat on a segregated bus.

DECEMBER 5, 1955 — Black people begin the Montgomery Bus Boycott.

FEBRUARY 1, 1960 — The Greensboro Four refuse to leave their seats at a Woolworth lunch counter and inspire other sit-ins.

MARCH 27, 1961 — Nine Black Tougaloo college students stage a sit-in at the segregated Jackson Municipal Public Library in Mississippi.

MAY 28, 1963 — Anne Moody, Memphis Norman, Pearlena Lewis, and other students and teachers from Tougaloo College stage a nonviolent protest at the Woolworth lunch counter in Jackson, Mississippi.

AUGUST 28, 1963 — Martin Luther King Jr. gives his famous "I Have a Dream" speech during the March on Washington.

JUNE 15, 1964 — The first group of volunteers arrived in Mississippi during Freedom Summer to help register Black voters.

PHOTO REFLECTION

What is your reaction to this photo? Have you ever been excluded from a place or event based on who you are or what you look like? Consider how your experience might be different from a classmate's.

Take or draw a picture of a place you like to go to in your community. In what ways is this place welcoming to all? How could it be more welcoming?

GLOSSARY

ACTIVIST: a person who fights for a cause or for change

BOYCOTT: a refusal to buy, go to, or use something, usually as a protest to show disapproval or force a change

DISCRIMINATION: unfair treatment of a particular group of people

INEQUALITY: not being equal

INJUSTICE: an act that is wrong or not fair

INTEGRATE: the practice of uniting people of different races in the cause of equal rights

LUNCH COUNTER: a counter in a store or restaurant where food is served

SEGREGATION: a legal system of forced separation, done specifically by race. In America, this was made by the people in power, which historically have been white men.

SOURCE NOTES

13   Mark Memmott, "Franklin McCain, One of 'Greensboro Four,'
      Dies," NPR, January 10, 2014, https://www.npr.org/sections
      /thetwo-way/2014/01/10/261384803/franklin-mccain-one-of
      -greensboro-four-dies.

21   Bernice Johnson Reagon, "Music in the Civil Rights Movement,"
      interview by Maria Daniels, WGBH-TV, PBS, July 2006,
      https://www.pbs.org/wgbh/americanexperience/features
      /eyesontheprize-music-civil-rights-movement/.

23   Margaret Renkl, "These Kids Are Done Waiting for Change,"
      New York Times, June 15, 2020, https://www.nytimes.com
      /2020/06/15/opinion/nashville-teens-protests.html.

24   Renkl.

READ WOKE READING LIST

Civil Rights Movement Facts for Kids
https://historyforkids.org/civil-rights-movement/

Collier, Bryan. *We Shall Overcome*. New York: Orchard Books, 2021.

Greensboro Sit-In
https://kids.britannica.com/students/article/Greensboro-sit
-in/632843

Long, Michael G. *Kids on the March: 15 Stories of Speaking Out, Protesting, and Fighting for Justice*. Chapel Hill, NC: Algonquin Young Readers, 2021.

Robinson, Sharon. *Child of the Dream: A Memoir of 1963*. New York: Scholastic, 2019.

SNCC: Student-Driven Civil Rights Activism
https://socialstudiesforkids.com/articles/ushistory/sncc.htm

Tyner, Dr. Artika R. *Black Lives Matter: From Hashtag to the Streets*. Minneapolis: Lerner Publications, 2021.

Youth in the Civil Rights Movement
https://www.loc.gov/collections/civil-rights-history-project
/articles-and-essays/youth-in-the-civil-rights-movement/

INDEX

PHOTO ACKNOWLEDGMENTS

Image credits: Bettmann Archive/Getty Images, pp. 4, 15, 18; Werner Bethsold/Wikimedia Commons (CC BY-SA 4.0), p. 5; AP Photo/HORACE CORT, p. 6; The Visibility Project, Claudette Colvin/Wikimedia Commons (Public Domain), p. 7 (left); Universal History Archive/Getty Images, p. 7 (right); Tullio Saba/Wikimedia Commons (CC BY-SA 4.0), p. 9; AP Photo/Tennessean, p. 10; Wally McNamee/CORBIS/Getty Images, p. 11; AP Photo, p. 12; AP Photo/Bob Jordan, p. 13; AP Photo/Gene Smith, p. 16; Courtesy of the Archives and Records Services Division, Mississippi Department of Archives and History, p. 17 (all); Bettmann Archive/Getty Images, p. 18; Library of Congress, p. 19; AP Photo/Jack Thornell, p. 20; Matt McClain/The Washington Post/Getty Images, p. 22; Photo by Amy Harris/Shutterstock, p. 23; Michal Urbanek/Shutterstock.com, p. 24; Delano, Jack/Wikimedia Commons (Public Domain); Cecily Lewis portrait photos by Fernando Decillis.

Cover: John Melton/Oklahoma Historical Society/Getty Images; David M. Schrader/Shutterstock.com; MilanoArt/Shutterstock.com.

Content consultant credit: Dr. Abdulai Iddrisu, associate professor of History and African Studies, Director of Africa and the African Diaspora at St. Olaf College

Lerner Publications Company
An imprint of Lerner Publishing Group, Inc.
241 First Avenue North
Minneapolis, MN 55401 USA

For reading levels and more information, look up this title at www.lernerbooks.com.

Main body text set in Aptifer Sans LT Pro.
Typeface provided by Linotype AG.

Editor: Brianna Kaiser **Designer:** Viet Chu **Photo Editor:** Giliane Mansfeldt
Lerner team: Martha Kranes, Sue Marquis

Library of Congress Cataloging-in-Publication Data

Names: Lewis, Cicely, author.
Title: Focus on civil rights sit-ins / Cicely Lewis.
Description: Minneapolis : Lerner Publications, [2023] | Series: History in pictures (Read woke books) | Includes bibliographical references and index. | Audience: Ages 9–14 | Audience: Grades 4–6 | Summary: "Although the institution of slavery ended with the US Civil War, racism persisted. Learn about Civil Rights Sit-Ins, the key figures who fought for equality, and the movement's connections to present day"— Provided by publisher.
Identifiers: LCCN 2021045376 (print) | LCCN 2021045377 (ebook) | ISBN 9781728423500 (library binding) | ISBN 9781728462851 (paperback) | ISBN 9781728461380 (ebook)
Subjects: LCSH: Civil rights movements—United States—History—20th century—Juvenile literature. | Civil rights demonstrations—United States—History—20th century—Juvenile literature. | Civil disobedience—Juvenile literature. | Protest movements—Juvenile literature.
Classification: LCC E185.615 .L47757 2023 (print) | LCC E185.615 (ebook) | DDC 323.0973—dc23

LC record available at https://lccn.loc.gov/2021045376
LC ebook record available at https://lccn.loc.gov/2021045377

Manufactured in the United States of America
1-49188-49319-11/5/2021